BLACK'S LAWS:

Chewable Theory You Won't Find in the Stacks

Jan Knippers Black

BLACK'S LAWS: Chewable Theory You Won't Find in the Stacks

ISBN: 9798876881649

PHILOSOPHY / Political

Cover and interior design by Orion Black, copyright owned by Jan Knippers Black.

Preface

One of the sources of my inspiration for writing this book was Grace Slick, lead singer for the Jefferson Airplane band. She said "If you want to tell them the truth, you'd better make them laugh."

An earlier source of such inspiration sprang from a Fulbright award experience in Ecuador in 1984. My objective, for which I explored far and wide around the country, was to see whether the multitude of development and charity organizations there were meeting their goals. I've always been hard to surprise, but the answer to this one knocked me off my feet. For the most part, results were not only disappointing; they tended to be the opposite of the intended.

As a former Peace Corps Volunteer (Chile 1962-64), I was particularly disappointed to find that the Ecuadorian Ministry of Agriculture was swarming with Peace Corps Volunteers. A major mantra of the Corps was that our job was to teach our hosts how to take our jobs from us. Alas, I found on this visit that the ministry was dependent on the volunteers, while locals were desperate for jobs. I complained to my now deceased husband, Dr. Martin Needler, that everything I was finding was paradoxical. "So," he said, "write about paradox." I have done so ever since.

My first book devoted to development was entitled "Development in Theory and Practice: Bridging the Gap" (1990). The second edition, subtitled "Paradigms and Paradoxes." (1999).

You'll find echoes of the "laws," particularly in the chapter here called "Gnawing on the Bone." It was so labeled because there, some of the more puzzling laws are explained or given examples. If they leave you head-scratching still, don't despair. I'll wrap up the book with some laughs.

By the time I finished my development books, I was overcome by the bad habit I now call "Black's Laws." All my books since have carried such laws, but likewise have all old, abandoned purses and overflowing desk drawers. In fact, I'm still churning out new ones – just can't seem to stop.

I must confess that I've been an academic – writer, editor, and professor – most of my life, and if any of you happen to learn something useful from this book, I'll be pleased. But these laws are not intended to be taken as the last laws of Moses on the mountain. I invite you to play with them, argue with them, even pick up my bad habit and make your own laws. Most of all I hope these laws will open up new perspectives – new ways of seeing things.

Finally, a new perspective you pick up might be disturbing to you. I can't help but notice that our country has stumbled over a lot of wrong turns, turns from which we should have learned. But don't imagine that I'm a pessimist, never mind a cynic. If I call attention to a Constitution falling off the wall, it is only in hope that someone will catch it before it hits the floor.

Americans of good will still have the advantages of truth and numbers. But numbers must be organized and energized by truth. And remember, it's not enough to speak truth to power if power is not listening or listening only by tapping our phones!

Black's "Laws" are original to Dr. Jan Knippers Black. This enterprise, however, owes everything to the efforts of my former students, especially Amy Clark and Barry Vesser, and my colleague, Carolyn Taylor Meyer. It has taken months of collection, compilation, and organization to turn a bright idea into a full-fledged, seven-chaptered, book.

Images from the collection of Jan Knippers Black including many original works of her own.

For your unwavering redheaded courage and compassion— for inviting us to challenge perspectives and to reach for the Constitution in its slide from the wall—for your tenacity, even as Death stood knocking impatiently at your door—we thank you, Jan, for this gift of your laws and laughter.

CHAPTER 1
HISTORY, POLITICS AND GOVERNMENT

It is impossible to complete a transition to democracy while an unrepentant tyrant hovers over the process.

There is a great difference between what it takes to deal with perverse individuals in a relatively benign system and to deal with a system that is itself perverse.

The more important the decision (like going to war), the fewer and the less well informed will be those involved in making it.

Like high-altitude bombers, ultimate decision makers in the Global Village rarely need be confronted by the consequences of their actions or inactions.

History is about gods and kings and warriors (the rest is women's studies).

If official history does not coincide with popular history, it's not history.

Only "official" truth can become official history. Until official history coincides with shared experience, the vulnerable dare not and the invulnerable need not assume that their experience has really become history.

How can you know where you're headed if you don't know where you've been?

Of course, a "coalition" of the unscrupulous, the opportunistic, the fearful, the ignorant, and the apathetic makes for an ominous obstacle. But such a coalition is a product of the reproductive system of inequity–a tainted product that can and must be recalled.

The "protection" of an inattentive public may become a protection racket.

Most social and political systems are underpinned by denial.

The perfect plausibility of policy failures makes them good cover for policy decisions.

In the power game there is no such thing as dropping out--only dropping under.

In truly democratic elections, all money is foreign.

Real democracy is most likely to be found where the money isn't; money attracts the wrong kind of people.

With the help of a great many adjectives (limited, tutelary, illiberal, etc.) democracy has become almost universal.

A conspiracy becomes a system when they all do it - and call it Professional Standards.

Partnership between a profit and a non-profit organization is like that between a pigeon and his statue.

In politics there is no steady state; if any rights are lost, those remaining become more difficult to defend.

It's a good bet that those who call for short-term sacrifice for the sake of long-term benefit are taking their cuts in the short term.

Criminal justice in the United States means crime against justice – assaults on the people may start with the young and poor and black or brown or female, but they don't stop there.

The admissibility of Smoking Gun evidence depends on who's standing behind the gun.

"Reasons of State" are the reasons some people have so much money and others have so little.

The role of government is not to mediate between private and public interest; it is to represent and advance the public interest.

Everybody favors democracy – that is, from the top of the food chain down to his or her place on that chain, not for those below.

The US regularly becomes polarized between those who would burn the flag and those who would burn the constitution.

The difference between the major parties in the United States is simple; the Democrats do with chagrin what the Republicans do with glee.

There is no such thing as bipartisan legislation. Any bill that passes the house, turns sharply to the right in the Senate. Republicans don't negotiate and Democrats do not hold their ground.

Ethnic chauvinism is a distraction. The leader who can claim a majority based on policy consensus doesn't need it.

A convincing candidate is one who is willing to lose.

The more costly and complicated a bill, the less time and attention will be allowed the congressional bodies expected to vote it up or down.

Congressional votes cast in haste to be lost in the crowd are often regretted in lonely retrospect.

Gambling is putting your money where your mouth is. Politics is putting your mouth where your money is.

Jan Knippers Black

Dictatorship is not one-man rule, but empowerment of bullies throughout the system.

Tyranny is an equal opportunity abuser; it "democratizes" abuse otherwise limited to the poor.

An elected civilian government in a straitjacket - a government unwilling or unable to act on a popular mandate- may be a better safeguard for inequity than a military dictatorship. (At least under dictatorship, people know they are being cheated.)

Abusive governments get away with denial because abused populations want denial, too.

An administration that sets out to prove that government doesn't work always succeeds.

"Could be worse" is not good enough when things could just as well be better.

Bipartisanship is a conspiracy of the elected against the electorate.

A ruling party need not seek to share credit, only blame.

A government lacking a serious opposition party or movement is a kleptocracy.

A "smoking gun" will not be picked up as long as its owner has more big guns. Official history screens out revelations opinion makers and the public are not prepared to entertain.

People who believe they have freedom of expression probably have not tried to use it.

Impotence also corrupts.

The game for those at the top of the social pyramid is to keep those at the bottom fighting among themselves.

All elected governments are ultimately centrist. A government launched from either end of the political spectrum is pulled toward the center as its term progresses.

A policymaker may become a statesman only when he is permanently out of the loop.

Reform can be achieved only at the expense of the reformer. Especially in small group politics, the initial challenger becomes the scapegoat in the denouement phase of acceptance of change.

The poorer the country, the more luxuriant the presidential palace; the less serious the function of legislators, the greater their perks.

There is an inverse relationship between the value of elections and the cost of candidacy. Would that "free elections" were.

When legislatures start gaining tenure, professors start losing it.

We know that unemployment has gotten out of hand when the state loses its job. "Democracy" poses no threat to elites when economic decision-making has been outsourced.

Mobile money means immobilized political leadership.

Academic disciplines were invented to keep professors talking past each other and to ensure that academic discourse never touches a nerve.

Dictatorship is a frame of mind---the vindication of an attitude, not one-man rule but a license that makes petty dictators out of everyone who serves the system.

The Right believes in the "power elite" but doesn't talk about it; the Left talks about the power elite but doesn't believe it (if they believed it, they'd know better than to talk about it).

The only effective balance of power is a balance between political and economic power--that is, the power of money and the power of organized people.

A liberal is one who is radical about the past, ambivalent about the present, and delusional about the future.

Politics is not a parlor game; it is the action at the top of the food chain.

Anybody who thinks there's plenty of room at the top hasn't tried to get there.

Buying candidates is not an improvement over buying votes; the latter at least gave something to the electorate, if only whiskey.

Globalization is the unfettering of capital at the expense of the fettering of government.

Where there are large gaps in wealth and power, adherence to law is optional for those at the top.

The mantle of office for elected leaders is a straitjacket. Election to office does not mean to power.

Jan Knippers Black

Power is the only protective mantle of office. The rituals and trappings that remain after power has been stripped serve only to make the naked emperor look colder.

Without extremists, there are no moderates. Moderates who play along with one extreme in the elimination of the other are suckers; they soon find themselves as a target extreme with no "moderates" to protect them.

Authority and responsibility are opposite ends of a seesaw; whenever one slips upward in the social strata, the other slips downward.

There is no general principle too sound, no religious or secular value too sacred to be used by the strong to abuse the weak. The only defense against abuse is de facto equality.

Politics is the art of marketing private interest as if it were the public interest or, conversely, of marketing the public interest as if it were cover for the private.

Mainstreams are monitored by big boats. Mainstreaming of an agenda or program should not be considered until its constituency has a well-armed navy.

Collective survival is the only kind.

Goliath cannot be killed with Goliath-sized stones; the stones must be David-sized so David can pick them up. (Big stones and big crimes may be unimaginable, but small stones and petty crimes cut a tyrant down to size.)

Jan Knippers Black

CHAPTER 2

ECONOMICS AND DEVELOPMENT

Politics and economics are inseparable; politics without economics is entertainment; economics without politics is religion.

There is an inverse relationship between the value of what one does and what one gets paid for doing it.

Comparative disadvantage is the inability to produce what one would consume, to consume what one produces, or to have any say about what is to be produced or consumed.

The economic model of the global village constitutes a synthesis of East and West: privatization of gains and socialization of losses.

Charity is a special tax on the caring.

In the non-profit world, a lot of non profit slips in.

Market forces are not forces of nature; they are just people who are able to avoid social responsibility.

Economists are prone to preface their assertions with "all else being equal" or "given a level playing field." But "all else" is never equal, and "level playing fields" are never given; they are won.

The rich North has exported to the poor South its production models, its consumption mania, its polluting technology, and its garbage. Now it seeks to export as well the blame for environmental degradation and the responsibility for reversing it.

Jan Knippers Black

We are all either carpetbaggers or migratory laborers now. Some can live anywhere they want to. Others just want a place to live. But all of us have lost our moorings.

Exploited outlanders, pouring into the metropolis as refugees, immigrants, or guest workers, eventually take over.

The laboratory for appropriate technology and sustainable development is usually the country that has no choice.

The indigenous were among the first native species depleted by explorers and exploiters superimposed over their homelands and the last to enjoy the rights of citizenship. They are also the only reliable guardians of their habitats, and perhaps, our planet.

To those who have been living for decades without wheels, a reinvented wheel is not unwelcome.

The quickest way to achieve high GNP growth rates in a relatively underdeveloped region is to harvest all the resources and replace the local people with rich foreigners.

Free trade is not about trade; it is about investment, and the cost to locals is ever-deepening debt.

An institute or corporation that frequently changes its name is probably admitting to failure, if not to crime.

If you're looking to hire a comer, bear in mind that a comer is also a goer.

Why do the high rollers fight fiercely against policy serving their own interest as well as the public interest? Perhaps it confirms that for some, prejudice trumps even greed.

The most insecure states, classes, and individuals are those that have the most to lose.

The rich pretend to know more than they do; the poor pretend to know less.

In the Global Village real prices are international, real wages are local.

When you see "Ethics" being taught in the business school, you know it's the end for ethics.

In economics and politics, experts get paid more for being wrong.

Species and cultures come to be valued only when they are almost extinct.

Corporations no longer compete for consumers but rather for investors/ stockholders and credit ratings, based not on product but on stock values.

Competition in the global marketplace is not so much between corporations as between localities, and the objective is to cut costs not prices.

Appropriate theory, like appropriate technology, need not be either old or new, high or low, simple or complex. It need only be accessible and useful to those who need it most.

The ultimate collateral in the case
of private loans to client states,
guaranteed by donor states, is the labor
of the peoples of both donor and client
states.

The eucalyptus economy features
transplanted high-yield ventures
with shallow roots that grow rapidly
by drawing off nutrients from their
surroundings, thus starving older native
species.

Streaker capital (e.g., portfolio) streaks
in and out of revolving doors of
eucalyptus economies.

The "informal sector" is not a reserve
category; it is everybody except the
relative few favored by the transplanted
modern economy. The informal sector
was "discovered" by economists in
the same sense in which Columbus
discovered America: It was there all
along.

If the trickle-down approach to economic redistribution fails, there is always mugging.

CEO's who beat the drums loudly about jobs are concerned first of all about their own.

Limited liability for the corporate world means unlimited liability for the rest of us.

The post-Cold War economic model constitutes a synthesis of East and West: privatization of gains and socialization of losses.

Privatizing usually means using public assets and public money to promote private interests. A government may nationalize failing enterprises (i.e. to bail out private owners), but it can privatize only successful or potentially successful ones.

Economics and religion have switched realms and roles, as between the physical and metaphysical and between legitimation of and confrontation with power. Economics have even taken over the miracle business.

Economic miracles, like religious ones, are most often about rising from the dead. Economic miracle makers have to destroy economies before they can resurrect them.

There is a built-in adjustment mechanism in the job market. When job loss becomes extreme, many who had worked in production, trade, and services will be hired back as policemen, security guards, and prison wardens.

Homelessness is not a consequence of poverty; the poorest communities take care of their own. It is a consequence of wealth poorly distributed.

If property is theft, intellectual property is delusion.

A partnership between the for-profit sector and the nonprofit sector is like the partnership between a con artist and his mark.

Bankers collect by hook or by crook. When creditors cannot collect from indigent borrowers, they collect instead from well-meaning innocents. Donations to debt relief for the poor are, in effect, reimbursements to lenders for debts they would otherwise have to write off.

The most addictive and abused narcotic on the market today is money; the system has a three-trillion-dollar-a-day habit–and will kill to maintain it.

A development agency that is not in trouble probably isn't doing its job. That is the case especially if the goal is empowerment, because power is relational---the prize in a zero-sum game.

It is easier to promote something new than, like Sisyphus, to keep pushing the same stone uphill. Maybe that's why the only development model older than time---community self-help---keeps being rediscovered and renamed.

International financial institutions have been remarkably successful in chasing away poverty---from the vicinity of their conference hotels.

A successful popular grass-roots organization will soon find a competitive and better-funded organization stealing its limelight and its constituency.

Evaluations have to be written, but they do not have to be read.

Responsibility shared is responsibility shunned. When it is spread across continents and hemispheres, scores of branch offices and bureaucratic levels, it becomes impossible to track.

Given a disjuncture between the objective and the capabilities and inclinations of the instrument, the latter always prevails.

The difference between charity and development is that charity builds dependency; development breaks it.

A set of people becomes a community when the whole is more than the sum of its parts.

Decision-making by "stakeholders" is a form of corporatism---a step forward from feudalism but a step backward from democracy.

The great appeal of diplomacy and development is that it is always easier to solve someone else's problems.

Appropriate theory, like appropriate technology, need not be either old or new, high or low, simple or complex. It need only be accessible and useful to those who need it most.

One of the requirements for reducing poverty and income gaps in the Third World is to reduce them in the First World. The First World countries that have been most serious about reducing poverty overseas are the ones that first committed to reducing it at home.

To every solution there is a problem.

Development programs are given impetus, not by underdevelopment, but by the fear of development that is not programmed by far away donors.

Credit is extended only to those who do not need it.

For states as for households, debts are less likely to get out of hand if the same folks who contract them and enjoy the benefits have to endure the hardships necessary to service them.

Risk capital is the kind invested in politicians; if those funds are invested well, other investments are insured.

Jan Knippers Black

When prescriptions are the same for patients with very different maladies, chances are the needs being met are those of the doctors.

For employees, "flexibility" means the right to work whenever the boss wants them to and to receive in payment whatever the boss wants to give them.

An economic theory that offers only the ahistorical promise of market-regulated trickle down in the long term is of little use to those waiting to be trickled on.

It's remarkable how stoically some (e.g., international bankers) can endure the pain of others.

The most vulnerable economies are not those with too little foreign capital but those with too much. An open door to foreign capital becomes a revolving door.

Globalization is not just about geography; it's about leaving nothing of value beyond the reach of the market. There ought to be something left that you can't buy: body parts, the presidency, or the right to pollute.

The laws of free-market economics are just another set of laws that the powerful are not obliged to obey.

CHAPTER 3
BUREAUCRACY & COMMUNICATIONS

Nothing succeeds like failure. Rather than admit to failure, a public agency will attribute deterioration of the situation to inadequate funding and solicit more.

Nothing fails like success. A successful community (as in drawing tourists), institution (as in drawing funds), or person (as in drawing celebrity) risks becoming a caricature.

A state lottery is a special tax on the stupid.

There is an inverse relationship between the social value of a task and the funds available to support it; likewise, an inverse relationship between the value of what one does and what one gets paid for doing it.

One who takes seriously the mandate a bureaucracy professes should be labeled an innocent or a rogue.

Words are prostitutes, for sale to the highest bidder.

Running a government like a business means underpaying workers and overcharging consumers and taxpayers in order to generate maximum profits and benefits for a few.

Any gain in comprehensiveness is offset by a loss in specificity. If you classify all documents or lock up all lawbreakers, the ones that shouldn't get out surely will.

If a representative of the king sits on the board, his vote constitutes a majority.

Any fool can sell what belongs to him. The trick, as governments and corporate cannibals are discovering, lies in selling off what belonged to others.

The poorer the people served, the poorer will be the bureaucracy and the bureaucrats who serve them.

Revenues earmarked for the non-affluent become a substitute for, rather than a supplement to, funds for that sector from the general operating budget.

The crucial issue is never whether to tax or spend or regulate but rather who to tax, who to regulate and who to spend on.

Research findings tend to reflect the interest of research funders. Those who would control policy must also control the research, analysis, and evaluations used to sell it.

Services and benefits limited to the poor are not sustainable politically. No service will be run at a high level of efficiency over a long period of time unless all classes are dependent on it (e.g., public education, health, transportation). That explains the enduring legacy of Social Security.

The ultimate in chutzpah is to deny to the other---for his own good---what one claims for oneself. For example, the U.S. military/Congress deny to the non-titled "socialism," subsidized services such as health care. Industrialized states deny industrialization. The secure deny security.

Treating the symptoms may prolong the disorder.

A government that consistently overborrows is undertaxing.

Good leadership is not defined by tight reins or loose ones, but by knowing who to rein in and who to let loose.

The nation-state system has become a state of denial.

In the new East, phones don't work because of outdated technology; in the West they don't work because of updated technology.

Government is a protection racket that doesn't deliver.

Professionalism is shared guilt. Like bipartisanship and multilateral operations, it provides collective justification for malfeasance.

The bathwater may or may not go, but when the throwing out starts, baby goes first. Lean and efficient government is an illusion. When government budgets are slashed, services are cut before salaries, and the first employees to be cut are the least well paid and the least readily expendable.

A government that calls for volunteerism is admitting defeat.

A government that shrinks from direct taxation will not simply close up shop; it will stop at nothing short of mugging people on the streets to raise revenue.

Both the war on drugs and the war on immigrants are wars of attrition, relying on body counts--a supply-side approach to a demand-driven problem.

Privatizing social security amounts to putting the winnings of almost a century of civilization on the roulette table and spinning the wheel.

Globalization does not necessarily mean that the government is shrinking, just that it has been outsourced.

Any fool can sell what belongs to him. The trick, as governments and corporate cannibals are discovering, lies in selling off what belonged to others.

Jan Knippers Black

He who pays the piper does not necessarily call the tune.

The size of the market for snake oil depends on the size of the snake pedaling it. Any theory is marketable if it is packaged with an adequate portion of carrots and sticks.

Purveyors of disinformation become convinced by their own propaganda.

Every good term deserves another. In public discourse, any term with a strongly positive connotation will soon be used to denote its opposite as well. Thus, a new term must be introduced to convey the original meaning.

A "gaffe" is the unintentional utterance of an uncomfortable truth. Only children and comedians get away with speaking the truth.

The less one has to say, the more likely one is to have a forum---and vice versa.

The primary role of a spokesperson is stonewalling.

The rationale for a policy initiative is usually the opposite of the reason for it; the rationale is intended to neutralize those who would otherwise oppose it. Thus, those who would maintain privilege must sell their proposals as essential to the public interest.

The first news is the worst news. Subjects tend to be introduced into public discourse by those whose interests are at stake. Especially in crisis situations, the first news, often taken from government press releases, is the least reliable.

Objectivity is achievable only by the mindless.

If they bother to deny it, it must be true.

The purpose of communications is to obscure misdeeds and motives. Thus, the communications superhighway is paved with fertilizer, and truth is roadkill.

Lightweight people and arguments float to the top.

An argument that cannot be made effectively on logical, ethical, or pragmatic grounds will be made on technical grounds or camouflaged in technicalese.

Those who are stingy with truth are sure to be defeated by those who are generous with lies.

The longer an agency has been in operation and the more eroded its functions, the greater the budget of its public relations department.

In journalism and scholarship, having the "right" sources and the wrong information is a lot safer than the other way around.

Computer simulation is the modern functional equivalent of reading tea leaves or gazing into crystal balls. Findings flow from the assumptions or needs of the programmers.

Truth is inconvenient to power.

High salaries normally amount to hush money.

The great value of truth lies in its rarity.

A social critic is a whistleblower on the system.

Modern media have greatly simplified the problems of conceptualization. Heroes and victims, the famous and the infamous, the outspoken and the outrageous all blur into the single concept of "celebrity."

Words are prostitutes---for sale to the highest bidder. Sovereignty came to mean license for governments to oppress their own peoples; culture: for men to abuse women; efficiency: for owners to exploit workers; development: for richer countries to drain poorer ones; globalization: for the private sector to suppress the public one; and free markets: for big business to gobble up small business.

CHAPTER 4

WAR, PEACE AND SECURITY

Peace is not simply the absence of war; but the absence of war might be a good place to start.

For a superpower, all wars are wars of choice.

Violence results from power inequalities. The only real solution to the problem of violence is empowerment of the would-be victims.

The only thing worse than losing a war is winning too big; either serves to glorify war.

War is expensive but always affordable; peace has to pay its own way.

There are no winners in wars of attrition, just losers in disproportionate numbers.

The Cold War was not to be another "war to end all wars." It was the war to end all peace; the War on Terrorism, the war to end all rights.

Security is a conceptual trump card, played always by those who have the most to lose rather than the most to fear.

Security as the problem implies force as the solution.

A people are only as secure as the most vulnerable in their midst.

Unconventional war is now the only kind that is conventional - bases and weapons and spies and troops all over the world. Conventional now means empire.

Jan Knippers Black

The more dramatic episodes of imposing or demonstrating imperial control, as in sending in the Marines, often appear to represent the deployment of weapons of mass distraction, undertaken more for their effect on the domestic power game - elections, opinion polls, or impending legislation--than for effect on the target country or region.

The most effective tactics for empire maintenance are played out day by day, year by year, almost automatically, below the radar screen, (as through universal surveillance and unnoticed censorship).

Just as a peace process requires the acknowledgment of crime and identification of individual criminals, the generation of wars requires collectivization of responsibility for individual crimes and dehumanization of whole populations.

Beheading alone will not kill the beast. Dictatorship is not the province of a lone tyrant. The example and implied impunity coming from the tyrant at the top empowers lesser tyrants throughout the system. Liberation will not be complete until they, too, have been swept back into the woodwork.

Identifying the disappeared may liberate survivors, but only identifying the abusers can liberate society.

All objects and ideas can be weaponized, and all weapons eventually fall into the wrong hands.

Terrorism represents a clash between criminals and honorable, law-abiding, and peace-loving people. It is not a clash of states, much less of civilizations, unless we choose to make it so.

In war there are political, bureaucratic, and corporate winners, but there are no

Forgiveness and reconciliation come more readily to the abused than to the abuser. Before he can "forgive" his victims, the abuser must first forgive himself. To do so, he must confront his own crimes. Until he can do that, he will project his guilt and remain dangerous to his former victims.

national winners, only losers in greater and lesser degrees.

In the war on terror, terror always wins.

There are no stakes too small for people to fight over.

Borders create aliens.

Forgiveness and reconciliation come more readily to the abused than to the abuser. Before he can "forgive" his victims, the abuser must first forgive himself. To do so, he must confront his own crimes. Until he can do that, he will project his guilt and remain dangerous to his former victims.

"Security" policies are designed by those who are objectively most secure--that is, by those nations, classes, and individuals who have the most to lose.

Most henhouses are guarded by foxes.

"Isms" are prone to be weaponized.

Martyrs are the creations of their enemies.

External leverage is crucial in prying open a closed system.

Most so-called wars are not wars at all, but episodic suppression of occupied peoples, and slow-moving genocide.

A bully-in-power does not attack other bullies, but rather journalists and scholars, musicians and other artists and pacifists who seek to inform and protect the vulnerable.

The strength of nationalism is in inverse proportion to the security of sovereignty.

Why is a peace process always more fragile, and easier to sabotage, than a war process?

There is a Catch-22 for modern-day Machiavellians: If they are fully successful in selling the cover story, they lose out to the true believers they created.

In the U.S. foreign affairs lexicon, liberals are true believers in development, conservatives true believers in empire, and moderates, or pragmatists, true believers in profit.

Security does not lie in a wall or a missile or a gun. It lies in the reasonable expectation of being able to maintain dignity and human connectedness from day to day.

The soviet system of workers against themselves as consumers left the majority frustrated and blaming the system. The U.S. system of each against all leaves a sizable minority in despair, blaming themselves.

When refugees are too numerous, rather than being protected by the system, they become protection for the system---enlightened politics and open markets.

Jan Knippers Black

Rich countries stay that way by taking in resources from poor countries but keeping the people out.

In all too many cases being a refugee has come to mean being imprisoned away from home.

An empire extends itself until it is overextended, thus bringing on its own demise.

CHAPTER 5
HUMAN RIGHTS

Whereas security is defined by those who have the most to lose, and "authoritative" commentary comes from those who have the most to hide, a human rights perspective reaches out and pays heed to those who have no spinmeisters, no official spokespersons or public relations teams, no layers of smoke and mirrors between their roles and their realities--and who, incidentally, without us may have no forum.

Like infectious disease, vulnerability moves up the social pyramid.

Before a people can chart its own future, it must reconstruct its past - that is, it must reinterpret a history fashioned by its oppressors.

Unlike the allocation of material goods, the allocation of rights is necessarily a zero-sum game, the status of which cannot be a status quo. If the categories of "humans" entitled and of rights respected are not expanding, they will be contracting.

The more extensive the categories of rights that are recognized and protected and the broader the categories of people covered, the greater will be our prospects of defending what we have and continuing to expand the frontiers.

Respect for human rights of certain people but not others, is just a matter of choosing sides.

Don't let people mistreat you; they will never forgive you for it. Forgiveness is easier for the abused than for the abuser. For the abuser, forgiving anyone, including himself, must begin with acknowledging guilt and assuming responsibility.

Jan Knippers Black

The human rights perspective and international human rights regime exist precisely because all else is not equal and because level playing fields are not given; they are won.

The struggle for respect for human rights is the last refuge of the human spirit.

An abuse is more clearly visible in historical perspective than unfolding right before you.

An abuse is more easily recognized by one who can identify more readily with the victim than the victimizer.

Human rights abuse is not necessarily illegal; many laws are in themselves abusive.

Abuse often accompanies and masquerades as misfortune.

To be recognized, an abuse must have a name.

Human rights abuse has many manifestations, but a single cause: inequality. Abusers abuse because they can.

Absence of complaint does not mean absence of abuse.

An abuse that comes to be routine will cease to be seen as an abuse.

Impunity is the measure of tyranny. It is the obverse of vulnerability, a license to abuse.

Human rights abuse has many manifestations, but a single cause: inequality. Abusers abuse because they can.

Abuse may be wholesale--as by terrorist states or occupation armies against whole nations; retail--targeting particular categories (racial or ethnic, women, workers); or selective--targeting individuals.

Abuse falls not only on the oppressed-- the unavoidably vulnerable--but also on the defenders of the oppressed.

Vulnerability is contagious. If one lacks
rights, all eventually do.

Rights may be individual, but protection
can only be collective.

Collective, or cultural, rights cannot
include the right of half the community
to abuse the other half.

Rights are won and lost in bunches;
the more rights a people loses, and
the more peoples who lose rights, the
harder it becomes to defend either
rights or peoples.

Religion enjoys the kind of "trump card"
status with respect to social and cultural
rights that "security" does with respect
to military matters.

If it is possible to do irreparable harm,
is it not also possible to do irreparable
good?

CHAPTER 6

GNAWING ON THE BONE

Protection is dangerous. The greatest danger to most people comes from their protectors (women from men, citizens from police, government from the military). Protection implies dependence, dependence implies inequality, and inequality invites violence.

Maintaining stability at the apex of the sharply graduated social pyramid requires perpetuating instability at the base--that is, keeping ethnic or political groups fighting among themselves.

When hardships are to be shared, the poor can count on getting more than their share; they can also count on a generous allotment of advice and blame.

Species and cultures come to be valued only when they are almost extinct. The last resort of an endangered species or embattled population is a high level of fertility.

Culture as explanation is a cover for ignorance. By attributing values and behaviors to culture, westerners are absolved from trying to understand and hence need only to overcome. Thus, culture as an explanation for underdevelopment leads not only to blaming the victims but also to suppression of the wellspring of regeneration and empowerment.

The more democratic the government, the higher the insurance premium it must pay to antidemocratic forces. To reassure merchants and mercenaries inclined to plot against governments

they can't control, political leaders beholden to the poor must be even more generous to the rich than their elitist adversaries.

Were it not for wrong reasons, there would be no right things done. The necessity of coalition building dictates that measures benefiting the powerless must appeal also to some sector of the powerful.

The more important the decision, the fewer and less well informed will be those involved in making it. Decisions viewed as most crucial to the system (e.g., war and peace) will be made by those having general responsibility and/or proximity to the ruler, rather than by those with expertise on the particulars of the crisis.

Those who pretend to promote democracy, human rights, or bottom-up development always run the risk of being successful.

The reigning development model since the 1990s is a modernized version of the cargo cult: build landing strips, golf courses, and sports stadiums (or garbage dumps and prisons); depress wages and declare tax holidays; and riches of exotic origin will drop on you.

Development programs are given impetus not by underdevelopment but by fear of uncontrolled development. As a rule, there is very little money for development until those who have the money and the power feel threatened-

--precisely by the self-activation of the poor.

The experts are always wrong. When one is working in an unfamiliar setting (and experts, by definition, are), the unexpected always happens. In fact, if development is to be sustainable the unexpected must happen---that is, the project must get "out of control" of the experts.

The failure of development---that is the perpetuation of poverty and inequity--- is a consequence not of policy failures but of policy decisions.

Saddling a project with secondary purposes may defeat its primary purpose, (If job creation is a secondary purpose in a construction project, the project can never be completed; workers must continually sabotage it.)

The more complex the plan or the technology, the more there is to go wrong.

The more money in the project, the more pages in the plan, the more certain the disaster. Money attracts scoundrels and encourages corruption, and complexity conceals the scams.

Low-income housing is never low enough.

The "feasibility" of a development project depends more on its paternity than on its promise.

Rural development is a process whereby affluent urban dwellers teach poor peasants how to survive in the countryside without money. All development programs and agencies are to some extent paternalistic.

The more important a development agency's mission and the more effective its performance, the sooner it will be suppressed. If an agency with an important mission, such as land reform, has any success at all, it will generate a reaction from the privileged classes. If it has no success, it will lose credibility among its supposed beneficiaries. Most likely, such agencies will generate reaction and lose credibility at the same time.

In the Third World, there is a need for technicians who are less well trained. For the most part, those who invest their time and money in acquiring professional status do not do so in order to work in muddy shoes.

Distance unites. Exploitation and racial and class discrimination may well be built into national and international systems, but their expression is local. Thus, changing traditional relationships may require the intervention of agents who are not local.

To every solution there is a problem. In development, as in politics generally, there are no happily-ever-afters. The "haves" will soon figure out how to turn any new law or program designed to

Were it not for wrong reasons, there would be no right things done. The necessity of coalition building dictates that measures benefiting the powerless must appeal also to some sector of the powerful.

benefit the "have-nots" to their own advantage. Thus, those who would promote the interests of have-nots cannot be caught napping.

Credit is extended only to those who do not need it. The lenders' interpretation of creditworthiness generally results in discrimination against those whose holdings and ambitions are modest. Even in microcredit programs, pressure is building to shun the poorest and move upmarket.

Sophistication in development processes is acquired and program continuity achieved not by donor institutions, but by individuals and client organizations. Objectives and approaches of major donor institutions shift in accordance with elite political climate rather than in response to experience or outcome in client states or communities.

Third World governments are weakened by the lack of pressures. Pressures on such governments are fierce and incessant, but they are virtually all from one side---the side of the rich. For long-term effectiveness, development programs must build up countervailing pressures.

Treating the symptoms may prolong the disorder. Programs that simply meet immediate needs rather than enable communities to meet their own needs are likely to kill local initiative and build dependency.

The primary beneficiaries of rural development programs are the cities. Development money becomes concentrated in the cities, where offices are maintained, supplies are purchased, and salaries are earned and spent.

The easiest way to solve a problem is to redefine it. Time was when doing without (austerity) and unemployment (the informal sector) were seen as the problems. Now they are being touted as the solutions.

The poor have always understood what the rich have not; that there is greater security in community than in cash.

He who pays the piper does not necessarily call the tune. Development is a complicated process, an art as much as a science, a creature of fortune as much as of planning, and no one, not even those who pay the bills, can control it.

CHAPTER 7
THAT'S LIFE

The path of least resistance lies in being radical about the past, ambivalent about the present, and delusional about the future.

With enough enlightenment, self-interest can be the functional equivalent of ethics.

Most things that seem too good to be true are.

The buck stops short.

Those who believe they have freedom of expression have not tried to use it

Truth is a lonely traveler, the bastard at every family picnic.

If we can't tell the difference between where we are and where we want to be, we're not going anywhere.

It is safer to be wrong forever than to be right too soon.

Important truths, escaping belatedly from the news, will never make it back to the front page.

As master of the spiritual realm, men have assumed responsibility for life after death and before birth; women only have to worry about the parts in between.

When two become one, it's generally one or the other.

The greater the risks and the smaller the rewards, the more likely it is that leadership roles will be held by women.

How many women does it take to change a light bulb? About one-third. For women to change anything, they must constitute one-third of the decision makers.

What the people don't know won't hurt the people who are hurting the people.

Consequences are always unintended.

If you go looking for trouble, you will find it.

If hypocrisy is the tribute that vice pays to virtue, we'd better invest it well.

What good could come of a day that starts with getting out of bed?

Be careful who you step on in your climb to fame and fortune. You're likely to meet them again on your way back down.

Pets are needed to humanize homes.

Ambitious fools are prone to say "Time is Money." Not so. Time is Life. Money is just stuff.

The long term is a product of the short term. One does not achieve equity in the long term by sacrificing it in the short term.

It doesn't matter where you start; what matters is which way you are headed. No matter where you are headed, you have to start from where you are. Having to start from where you are means having to recognize where you are.

Until 18 and after 80, a lady might be escorted across the street, but through the "middle ages," she has to make it on her own.

Given the cost and all the paperwork, dying is hardly worth the trouble.

Real power is not an attribute of a role, but rather of personal character.

Unscrupulousness ought to count for something.

Ordinary People are rarely ordinary.

Just as robots are learning to talk and act like humans, humans are learning to talk and act like robots.

Creativity is not a skill set, but a mindset.

The quickest way to lose a forum is to make use of it.

There is no such thing as "opting out." There are only two ways to relate to the power system: as subject or as object-- participant or victim.

Opportunities ordinarily go to opportunists.

Being right too soon is more damaging to a career than being right too late.

Things can always get worse.

Without idealism one has no destination. Without ideology, no

anchor. Without pragmatism, no rudders.

Never trust anybody who is not aware that you can do him in.

I am not a pessimist; I am an optimist starting from a low base camp.

Thinking for oneself is always an act of defiance.

There are no happy-ever-afters, but there are ideas whose time comes around again and again, and some seem to come around stronger each time.

If it is possible to do irreparable harm, might it not also be possible to do irreparable good (e.g., to devise the policy, create the organization, leave the record, write the book or the song or the phrase that won't die)?

One must know the future in order to predict the past; history is periodically reconstructed to meet the needs of new power holders.

The future is not what it used to be. To get back to the future---the Age of Aquarius-envisioned in the 1960s and 1970s, we must recover lost road maps, paradigms interpreting the past and the potential of civilization.

In matters social and political, there is no such thing as the status quo; if things aren't getting better, they're getting worse.

Friendship is an expendable resource; the more of it you use, the less you keep.

The sincerest expression of appreciation is a fat paycheck.

It is dangerous to make waves when you are in a small boat.

Success is in sync with particulars of time and place. Greatness rises above them.

Debts of gratitude are generally defaulted.

In the age of artificial intelligence and virtual culture, we are more than ever in need of real values.

Knowing who you are makes it easier to identify your enemies.

Wisdom does not travel on the fast track; by the time it catches up with

Be careful who
you step on
in your climb
to fame and
fortune. You're
likely to meet
them again on
your way back
down.

you, you've nothing to do with it except pass it on.

Attending to a problem is not the same as solving it.

The unthinkable will remain unthunk so long as the Big Lie trumps the Big Truth.

Social learning can become general and effective only when options are apparent and people are prepared to deal with the consequences of what they dare to know.

Do the right thing; just don't get caught at it.

Success is in sync with particulars of time and place. Greatness rises above them.

Debts of gratitude are generally defaulted.

In the age of artificial intelligence and virtual culture, we are more than ever in need of real values.

Knowing who you are makes it easier to identify your enemies.

Wisdom does not travel on the fast track; by the time it catches up with you, you've nothing to do with it except pass it on.

Attending to a problem is not the same as solving it.

The unthinkable will remain unthunk so long as the Big Lie trumps the Big Truth.

Social learning can become general and effective only when options are apparent and people are prepared to deal with the consequences of what they dare to know.

Do the right thing; just don't get caught at it.

About the Author

Dr. Jan Knippers Black is a globally recognized expert on Latin America, its political dynamics, and the relationships of its countries to the United States; she is also a world-renowned scholar and advocate for the cause of human rights, as well as a prolific author.

With a Bachelor of Arts in Art and Spanish from the University of Tennessee, a Master's in Latin American Studies from the School of International Service and a PhD in International Studies, both from American University, Jan was among the first generation of Peace Corps volunteers to serve in Chile. Judge Juan Guzmán Tapia, prosecutor of Chilean dictator Augusto Pinochet, in reference to Jan's book The Politics of Human Rights Protection remarked that hers is: "A stark and powerful portrayal of the wide panorama of rights under challenge, drawing lessons particularly from circumstances in which justice has prevailed over impunity."

Jan served as research professor in the Division of Public Administration, University of New Mexico; Editor and Research Administrator in American University's Foreign Area Studies Division; and a faculty member in the University of Pittsburgh's Semester-at-Sea Program. She held Fulbright, Mellon, and other grants; fellowships;

and visiting and honorary faculty positions in Latin America, the Caribbean, and India, as well as a senior associate position at St. Antony's College, Oxford University. Jan served two terms on the Board of Directors of Amnesty International USA. As a member of the Democratic Party, Jan also served on the Monterey County Democratic Central Committee and as an elected member of the Executive Board of the California Democratic Party for over 20 years.

Jan passed in August of 2021 after a tenacious struggle with cancer. Her loss was felt by all who knew her, but particularly her former students, the human rights community, and her colleagues all over the world working for justice.

Donations in Jan's memory may be made to the Jan Knippers Black Fund for Human Rights at the Middlebury Institute of International Studies, at www.engage.middlebury.edu.

Other Works
by Jan Knippers Black

The Politics of Human Rights Protection

Inequity in the Global Village:Recycled Rhetoric and Disposable People

The Dominican Republic: Politics and Development in an Unsovereign State

Sentinels of Empire: The United States and Latin American Militarism

United States Penetration of Brazil